Digital Marketing for Small Business Owners

Practical Strategies to Increase Online Visibility and Drive Sales

Dr. Miles J. Cooper

Disclaimer

This book, Digital Marketing for Small Business Owners: Practical Strategies to Increase Online Visibility and Drive Sales, is intended for informational and educational purposes only. While every effort has been made to ensure the accuracy and reliability of the content, the author and publisher make no guarantees regarding specific results or outcomes.

The strategies and techniques discussed are based on general industry practices and may not be suitable for all businesses. Readers are encouraged to adapt the information to their unique circumstances and consult professionals, such as marketing professionals or legal advisors, when necessary.

The author and publisher disclaim any liability for any losses or damages arising from the use of this book or its contents. Success in digital marketing depends on a variety of factors, including individual effort, market conditions, and external variables beyond the scope of this book.

By using this book, you acknowledge and agree to accept full responsibility for the decisions and actions you take based on its content.

All rights reserved. No part of this publication may be reproduced, distributed, or transmitted in any form or by any means, including photocopying, recording, or another electronic or mechanical method without the prior written permission of the publisher except in the case of brief citation embodied in critical reviews and certain other noncommercial use permitted by copyright law.
Copy right @Dr. Miles J. Cooper

Table of content

Part 1: Laying the Groundwork for Digital Marketing Success

Chapter 1: Understanding Digital Marketing
Chapter 2: Setting Clear Marketing Goals
Chapter 3: Knowing Your Audience

Part 2: Building A Strong Online Presence

Chapter 4: Crafting Your Brand Identity Online
Chapter 5: Creating An Effective Internet website
Chapter 6: Leveraging Local SEO

Part 3: Driving Traffic To Your Internet website

Chapter 7: Content Marketing Basics
Chapter 8: Social Media Marketing
Chapter 9: Search Engine Marketing (SEM)
Chapter 10: Email Marketing for Small Businesses

Part 4: Converting Visitors Into Customers

Chapter 11: Optimizing Your Sales Funnel
Chapter 12: Crafting High-Converting Landing Pages
Chapter 13: The Power of Online Reviews And Testimonials

Part 5: Sustaining Long-Term Success

Chapter 14: Analyzing Information And Adjusting Strategies
Chapter 15: Managing Your Marketing Budget
Chapter 16: Scaling Your Digital Marketing Efforts

Conclusion

Part 1: Laying the Groundwork for Digital Marketing Success

Chapter 1: UNDERSTANDING DIGITAL MARKETING

Digital marketing has generally changed how businesses connect with their customers. In this present reality where online presence can represent the moment of truth of a business, understanding the force of digital marketing is as of now not discretionary. It is fundamental. This section will investigate what digital marketing is, the reason it makes a difference, and how small businesses can use it for progress.

What is Digital Marketing, Why Does It Matter?
At its center, digital marketing is the utilization of the internet and online platforms to advance and sell items or services. This envelops a large number of strategies, for example, online marketing, email marketing, search engine optimization (Search engine optimization), content creation, and paid publicizing, all pointed toward arriving at potential customers where they invest the vast majority of their energy — on the internet.

Digital marketing is particularly significant for small companies because it makes everything fair. It offers the capacity to rival bigger businesses that might have further pockets for customary publicizing strategies. With digital marketing, a small business can contact a international audience, construct brand awareness, conduct people to its website, and finally believe that traffic into Sales — all while working with a more modest budget.

The requirement for digital marketing is highlighted by moving buyer ways of behaving. Like never before, customers depend on digital channels to find items, research businesses, and go with buying choices. On the off chance that your business is absent in the digital space, you're probably passing up amazing chances to draw in and hold customers.

Key Advantages for Small Businesses
Digital marketing offers many advantages that are especially worthwhile for entrepreneurs:
1. Practical Marketing: Dissimilar to conventional marketing channels like print advertisements or television plugs, digital marketing offers reasonable arrangements. Pay-per-click promotions, social media campaigns, and email marketing are many times more budget well-disposed than their customary partners, making them ideal for businesses with restricted assets.

2. Designated Reach: One of the main benefits of digital marketing is its capacity to target explicit audiences. With apparatuses like Google Advertisements and Facebook Promotions, entrepreneurs can unequivocally define their objective market in light of socioeconomics, interests, and online ways of behaving. This guarantees marketing dollars are spent all the more effectively, arriving at just the people who are probably going to draw in with your item or administration.

3. Quantifiable Outcomes: With customary marketing, measuring the progress of a campaign can be a challenge. Digital marketing, then again, gives information-driven experiences. You can follow website traffic, commitment levels, transformation rates, and profit from business (return for capital invested), permitting you to refine your strategies progressively. This straightforwardness guarantees that you can pursue informed choices and persistently further develop your marketing endeavors.

4. Building Brand Loyalty: Through digital marketing, businesses have more chances to draw in their customers. Whether it's through normal email bulletins, intelligent social media posts, or customized website content, digital marketing permits businesses to make significant partnerships with their audience, cultivating loyalty and rehashing business.

5. International Reach: Dissimilar to local, customary marketing techniques, digital marketing separates geological hindrances. A very much optimized online presence can assist small businesses with extending their arrival past their local region and accessing customers from around the world. This opens up new income streams and amazing learning experiences.

Outline OF Digital marketing CHANNELS

Digital marketing is an umbrella term that incorporates different channels, each offering unmistakable benefits. As an entrepreneur, understanding the various channels will permit you to pick the ones that line up with your business goals and target market. Here is a short outline of the most regularly utilized digital marketing channels:

1. Search engine optimization (SEO): Search engine optimization is the most common way of enhancing your website to rank higher in internet crawler results pages (SERPs). By executing the right keywords, making significant content, and upgrading the specialized parts of your website, you can work on your natural visibility on internet crawlers like Google. Search engine optimization is a drawn-out technique that can yield huge returns by driving free, natural traffic to your website.

2. Content Marketing: Content marketing includes making and sharing important content —, for example, blog entries, videos, internet casts, and infographics — that draws in and teaches your main interest group. The objective isn't to sell straightforwardly, yet to give information that forms trust and assists likely customers with pursuing informed choices. A top notch content technique can further develop Search engine optimization and conduct people to your website.

3. Social media Marketing: Social media platforms like Facebook, Instagram, LinkedIn, and Twitter offer a strong method for coming to and connect with your audience. Through natural content and paid marketing, businesses can associate with their audience, build brand awareness,

and drive Sales. Social media marketing likewise works with customer assistance, permitting businesses to address customer inquiries continuously.

4. Email Marketing: Email marketing is one of the best ways of sustaining partnerships with your customers. By sending customized, significant content to your email show, you can keep your audience connected, advance exceptional offers, and empower rehash buys. With computerization instruments, email marketing can be profoundly proficient, permitting businesses to send the ideal message brilliantly.

5. Pay-Per-Click Marketing (PPC): PPC advertisements, similar to research Promotions, permit businesses to offer keywords and show promotions to customers who look for those terms. In contrast to SEO, where results are acquired over the long run, PPC gives prompt visibility. While it requires a business, PPC can be an extraordinary method for driving traffic rapidly and producing Sales.

6. Affiliate Marketing: Affiliate marketing is an exhibition-based marketing procedure where businesses pay outsider accomplices (members) a commission for creating Sales or leads. This channel functions admirably for businesses hoping to grow their compass without putting resources into extra marketing assets.

7. Leverage Marketing: By cooperating with forces to be reckoned with who have a critical continuing in your specialty, you can use their validity and reach to advance your items or services. Leverage marketing is especially compelling in businesses like design, magnificence, and wellness, however, it tends to be applied to any business that needs to build brand awareness and trust.

8. Online Public Marketing (PR): Digital PR includes dealing with your business' online standing through media arrangements, public statements, and joint efforts with leverages. The positive online press can fundamentally optimize your brand's validity, further develop your Internet optimization rankings, and attract people to your website.

Why Private Businesses Need Digital Marketing Now Like Never Before
The conventional approaches to carrying on with work are presently sufficiently not. The pandemic and changing buyer inclinations have sped up the shift to internet shopping and digital commitment. Indeed, even in the post-pandemic world, this digital change keeps on reshaping the commercial center.
For small businesses, digital marketing isn't simply a discretionary marketing procedure — it's a fundamental device for endurance and development. As the digital scene develops, businesses that embrace new marketing strategies will be better situated to contend and succeed.

However, understanding digital marketing isn't just about having a website or being active via social media. It's about decisively utilizing on the internet apparatuses to improve your brand's visibility, interface with your audience, and at last, develop your business. The conducts examined in this part will be investigated in more profundity all through the book, furnishing you with the information and devices to make an effective digital marketing strategy for your small business.

CHAPTER 2: SETTING CLEAR MARKETING GOALS

Successful digital marketing starts with an unmistakable comprehension of your targets. Without distinct objectives, it's not difficult to sit around and assets on exercises that yield practically no return. For entrepreneurs, each work matters, and setting clear, significant marketing objectives guarantees that your strategies line up with your more extensive business goals. This section investigates the significance of defining Smart objectives, how to adjust marketing endeavors to business needs, and the role of key performance indicators (KPIs) in following achievement.

Significance OF Defining Brilliant Objectives

Marketing without a guide resembles exploring a new city without headings — it's wasteful, baffling, and improbable to prompt achievement. Objectives give construction and clearness when conducting your marketing endeavors toward quantifiable results. Nonetheless, not all objectives are made equivalent. This is where the Brilliant system becomes an integral factor.

Smart represents:
Explicit: Objectives ought to state what you intend to accomplish. Unclear goals like "increment Sales "are less noteworthy than "increment online Sales by 20% in a half year."

Quantifiable: Quantifiable targets permit you to follow progress and assess achievement. For example, measuring website traffic or social media commitment assists you with evaluating whether your campaigns are working.

Reachable: While aspiration is fundamental, your objectives ought to be sensible given your assets, time, and budget.

Applicable: Objectives ought to line up with your general business technique. Assuming that your essential goal is to build brand awareness, center around measurements like social media devotees or website impressions, not immediate Sales.

Time-Bound: Setting a cutoff time makes direness and responsibility, guaranteeing that your marketing endeavors keep focused.

By defining cost-effective objectives, you explain what achievement resembles as well as lay out an establishment for arranging and performance.

Step-By-Step Instructions to Adjust Marketing Strategies to Business Targets

Digital marketing objectives shouldn't exist in disengagement. They should uphold the more extensive goals of your business. For instance, assuming your essential business objective is to increment income, your marketing endeavors ought to zero in on driving Sales through designated crusades, upgrading your website for transformations, and sustaining leads through email marketing.

To guarantee arrangement, think about the accompanying advances:

1. Recognize Your Key Business Targets: Begin by framing your first concerns — whether it's rising brand awareness, sending off another item, holding existing customers, or venturing into new business sectors.

2. Map Marketing Strategies to Every Goal: Every business goal ought to have a comparing marketing technique. For example, on the off chance that you expect to draw in new customers, center around lead age strategies like internet crawler marketing (SEM) and content creation.

3. Focus on Given Effect: Private businesses frequently have restricted assets, so focus on systems that offer the most elevated expected profit from investment (return on initial capital investment). For instance, assuming your audience is profoundly active on Instagram, putting resources into social media campaigns might be more significant than paid search advertisements.

4. Include Your Group: On the off chance that you have a group, guarantee everybody comprehends how their errands add to general objectives. This cultivates coordinated effort and guarantees consistency across all marketing channels.

At the point when your digital marketing endeavors are in a state of harmony with your business targets, you formulate a strong procedure that drives quantifiable outcomes and expands effectiveness.

Tracking Success with KPIs

Defining objectives is just the initial step. To decide if your endeavors are viable, you want to follow progress utilizing key performance indicators (KPIs). These are quantifiable measurements that give experiences into how well your marketing techniques are performing.

What Makes a Decent KPI?

Significant: Pick KPIs that straightforwardly connect with your objectives. For instance, if you want to increment email commitment, track open and navigate rates.

Actionable: KPIs ought to give information that assists you with settling on informed choices. For example, on the off chance that your bob rate is high, it could demonstrate issues with your internet composition's or content.

Opportune: Consistently monitor KPIs to recognize drifts and change strategies depending on the situation.

Instances of Normal KPIs

1. Website Measurements:
-Traffic: Number of guests to your website, sectioned by source (e.g., natural, paid, social).
-Bob Rate: Level of guests who leave your website without making any move.
-Change Rate: Level of guests who complete an ideal activity, like making a buy or pursuing a pamphlet.

2. Social media Measurements:
-Commitment Rate: Likes, remarks, and offers comparative with the quantity of devotees.
-Adherent Development: The expansion in your social media audience over the long run.
-Impressions and Reach: Number of times your content is shown and the number of special customers that see it.

3. Email Marketing Measurements:
-Open Rate: Level of beneficiaries who open your email.
-Active clicking factor (CTR): Level of beneficiaries who click on a connection inside the email.
-Withdraw Rate: Level of beneficiaries who quit your email list.

4. Publicizing Measurements:
-Cost Per Snap (CPC): The sum spent per click on a promotion.
-Active visitor clicking percentage (CTR): The proportion of customers who click on your promotion to the people who see it.
-Return on Promotion Spend (ROAS): Income created from your advertisements contrasted with the sum spent.

Utilizing Information to Streamline Your Endeavors

Following KPIs isn't just about social event information — it's tied in with utilizing that information to further develop your marketing strategies. Consistently review your measurements and pose inquiries like:
-Is it true or not that we are meeting our objectives? If not, why?
-Which techniques are driving the most commitment, traffic, or Sales?
-Are there any failing to meet expectations regions that need change?

For instance, in the event that your email open rates are low, you could explore different avenues regarding different titles or sending times. In the event that your website's skip rate is high, consider further developing the customer experience by improving on route or making the content really captivating.

Defining clear marketing objectives is the foundation of an effective digital marketing system. By utilizing the Brilliant structure, adjusting your endeavors to business goals, and following advancement through KPIs, you guarantee that each activity you take adds to quantifiable outcomes.

The subsequent platform is to plunge further into understanding your audience — in light of the fact that realizing who you're attempting to reach is similarly essentially as significant as defining what you're attempting to accomplish. With clear objectives and a strong comprehension of your objective market, you'll be well headed to digital marketing achievement.

CHAPTER 3: KNOWING YOUR AUDIENCE

Understanding your audience is the foundation of any fruitful digital marketing system. For entrepreneurs, the capacity to interface with your objective market can mean the distinction between flourishing and simply getting by. This part will conduct you through the basics of distinguishing your objective market, making definite customer personas, and understanding online buyer conduct to guarantee your marketing endeavors resound with the perfect individuals.

Recognizing Your Objective Market

Before you can really market your items or services, you really want to define who your ideal customers are. An objective market is a particular gathering probably going to buy your contributions. Recognizing this gathering assists you with centering your assets and designing your marketing strategies to address their issues.

Moves toward Distinguish Your Objective Market:
1. Analyze Your Current Customers:
Begin by inspecting your ongoing customer base. Search for shared traits like socioeconomics, buying conduct, and inclinations. For instance, on the off chance that your best customers are ladies aged 25-40 who esteem eco-accommodating items, that is an unmistakable beginning platform.
2. Assess Your Contributions:
Contemplate the issues your items or services settle. Who benefits the most from your answers? Understanding the trouble spots you address can assist you with reducing your audience.
3. Concentrate on Your Rivals:
Exploring contenders can give important bits of knowledge. Who are they focusing on? What marketing strategies would they say they are utilizing? While you would rather not copy their strategy, gaining from their triumphs and disappointments can refine how you might interpret your own audience.
4. Section Your Market:
Partition your audience into more modest fragments in view of elements like age, orientation, area, interests, and pay level. This division considers more customized marketing efforts.

Making Customer Personas

Whenever you've recognized your objective market, the subsequent platform is to make customer personas. A customer persona is a semi-fictitious portrayal of your ideal customer in view of information and experiences. Personas rejuvenate your audience, assisting you with figuring out their inspirations, requirements, and ways of behaving.

Parts of a Customer Persona:
1. Socioeconomics:

-Age, orientation, marital status
-Training level and occupation
-Pay level and geographic area

2. Psychographics:
-Values, interests, and leisure activities
-Difficulties or trouble spots
-Objectives and desires

3. Social Experiences:
-Purchasing propensities and active cycles
-Favored correspondence channels (email, social media, and so on.)
-Online exercises, like perusing or shopping propensities

Illustration of a Customer Persona:
-Name: Sarah Green
-Age: 34
-Occupation: Marketing Conductor
-Objectives: To find eco-accommodating home items that line up with her qualities.
-Challenges: Restricted opportunity to explore items; overpowered by decisions.

Favored Channels: Instagram and email pamphlets.
Making 2-3 itemized personas can assist you with creating marketing emails that talk straightforwardly about your audience's necessities and inclinations.

Figuring out Online Buyer Conduct

In the present digital-first world, buyer conduct has developed essentially. Buyers explore, think about, and buy items on the internet, frequently across different platforms. To actually connect with your audience, you should comprehend how they settle on buying choices in the digital space.

Key Parts of Online Buyer Conduct:

1. The Buyer's Journey:
The buyer's process comprises of three phases:
-Awareness: The customer acknowledges they have an issue or need.
-Thought: They investigate choices and analyze arrangements.
-Choice: They pick an item or administration and make a buy.

Your marketing systems ought to take care of each platform. For example, blog entries or instructive contents function admirably during the awareness platform, while testimonials and reviews are essential during the choice platform.

2. Impact of Reviews and Social Verification:
Online buyers vigorously depend on reviews and proposals. As indicated by late analysis, 93% of shoppers say online reviews impact their buying choices. Empowering fulfilled customers to leave reviews and exhibit testimonials on your website can essentially affect trust and changes.

3. Mobile Shopping Patterns:
A huge level of internet shopping presently occurs on cell phones. Guaranteeing your website is active and offers a consistent shopping experience is basic to catching this audience portion.

4. Inclination for Personalization:
The present buyers anticipate customized encounters. From email proposals given to past buys to designated promotions, personalization can support commitment and drive Sales.

5. Effect of Social Media:
Social platforms play a huge part in forming purchasing choices. Numerous customers find new items on Instagram, Facebook, or Pinterest. Engaging with your audience through outwardly engaging and intelligent content on these platforms is fundamental.

Understanding where your listeners might be coming from is not a one-time task — it's a continuous cycle. As business sectors develop and customer inclinations shift, persistently refreshing the comprehension you might interpret your audience guarantees your marketing strategies stay powerful.

By recognizing your objective market, making itemized customer personas, and understanding internet-based buyer conduct, you set up significant partnerships and effective marketing efforts. With this strong groundwork, you're prepared to continue building areas of strength for a presence — the following basic move toward your digital marketing business.

Part 2: Building a Strong Online Presence

CHAPTER 4: CRAFTING YOUR BRAND IDENTITY ONLINE

A solid, predictable brand character is the foundation of powerful digital marketing. It's how your small business stands out in a jam-packed online commercial center, forms trust, and interfaces with your ideal interest group. Making your brand identity is something beyond designing a logo; it includes making a firm and paramount presence that imparts your business values and vision. This part investigates the significance of consistency in branding, designing proficient brand materials, and laying out a novel brand voice and message.

Significance of Consistency in Branding

Brand consistency implies guaranteeing that all parts of your business — from your logo and website to your social media posts — convey a firm and bound-together message. This consistency makes acknowledgment and trust, two fundamental components for driving customer unwaveringness.

Why Consistency Matters:
1. Acknowledgment and Review:
A reliable brand identity assists customers with effectively perceiving your business across various platforms. At the point when they see your logo or hear your slogan, they ought to promptly connect it with your contributions.
2. Trust and Amazing skill:
Individuals are bound to believe brands that seem coordinated and proficient. Steady branding signals that you are solid and focused on your business.
3. Enhanced Customer Experience:
Consistency guarantees that customers know what's in store for your brand, whether they're visiting your website, cooperating via social media, or getting an email.
4. Separation:
In a serious market, areas of strength for a predictable brand helps put you aside from contenders. It highlights what makes your business novel.

Designing A Professional Logo and Brand Materials

Your logo is much of the time the principal cooperation customers have with your brand. It's a visual portrayal of your business and ought to be noteworthy, proficient, and lined up with your general brand identity.

Ways to design a Viable Logo:
1. Straightforwardness is Vital:

A straightforward design is simpler to perceive and recall. Consider notable logos like Nike's swoosh or Apple's apple.

2. Color Psychology:
Pick colors that resound with your interest group and mirror your brand values. For instance, blue conveys trust and impressive skill, while green recommends eco-agreeableness and wellbeing.

3. Versatility:
Guarantee your logo takes a gander at any size, from a little favicon on your website to a huge standard on a board.

4. Timeless Design:
Stay away from patterns that might become obsolete. Go for the gold that will stay significant long into the future.

Other Fundamental Brand Materials:
-Business Cards: Even in the digital age, business cards remain a strong systems administration device. Keep the design clean, with your logo, contact information, and website URL.
-Social Media Designs: Make layouts for posts, standards, and profile pictures that line up with your brand tones and textual styles.
-Bundling (if applicable): Assuming you sell actual items, your bundling ought to mirror your brand character and optimize the customer experience.

For entrepreneurs without design ability, reasonable apparatuses like Canva or proficient creators on platforms like Fiverr can assist with making clean materials.

Laying Out Your Brand Voice and Message

Your brand voice is how your business speaks with its audience. It mirrors your character, values, and the general tone of your information. A clear-cut brand voice guarantees that each connection, whether through email, social media, or customer service, feels credible and predictable.

Instructions to Define Your Brand Voice:

1. Understand Your Audience:
Consider the inclinations and assumptions for your objective market. For instance, a brand focusing on youthful grown-ups could take on a relaxed and popular tone, while a brand taking special care of professionals could favor a formal and legitimate tone.

2. Mirror Your Qualities:
Your voice ought to line up with your business' fundamental beliefs. On the off chance that manageability is a key worth, your informing could stress eco-accommodating practices and socially cognizant language.

3. Be Credible:
Credibility assembles trust. Your brand voice ought to feel certifiable, not constrained or excessively prearranged.

4. Make a Style Guide:
Record your brand voice in a style guide. Incorporate instances of favored language, tone, and expressions, as well as words or styles to keep away from.

Creating Your Brand Message:

Your brand message conveys the pith of your business — what you do, why you make it happen, and how you help your customers. A convincing message resounds with your audience and motivates activity.

-Illustration of a Brand Message Format:
-What Your identity is: We are a family-claimed bread kitchen.
-What You Do: We make distinctive, natural bread and cakes.
-Why You Make it happen: We accept everybody merits top caliber, healthy heated merchandise.

Whenever you've defined your message, guarantee it's integrated into your website, marketing materials, and customer connections.

Consistency in branding, proficient design, and an unmistakable, credible voice cooperate to make a strong brand identity. This identity draws in customers as well as makes them want more.

Carve out opportunity to define and archive your brand components. Use apparatuses and assets that line up with your budget to make materials that mirror your incredible skill. Keep in mind, a durable brand identity is the establishment for building trust, acknowledgment, and dependability in the digital space.

By making areas of strength for a presence, you'll be exceptional to move into the following period of digital marketing achievement: making a successful website that fills in as the center of your online exercises.

CHAPTER 5: CREATING AN EFFECTIVE INTERNET WEBSITE

Your website is the digital retail facade of your business. It's generally expected the initial feeling potential customers have of your brand, making it a basic part of your online presence. A very much designed website draws in guests as well as keeps them drew in and guides them toward making a move, whether it's making a buy, pursuing a pamphlet, or reaching you for services.

In this section, we'll investigate the fundamentals of a small business website, tips for easy to understand design and route, and how to streamline your website for both versatile customers and internet search tools.

Basics of a Small Business Website

A powerful website for a small business needn't bother to be excessively complicated, yet it should fill its essential need: to illuminate, draw in, and convert guests.

Key Elements of an Effective Small Business Website:
1. A Clear Purpose:
Your website ought to quickly impart what your business does and how it can help guests. Utilize a compact slogan or title on your landing page to highlight your exceptional incentive.
2. Proficient Design:
Visual allure matters. Put resources into a spotless, present-day design that mirrors your brand character. Pick a variety design, typography, and symbolism predictable with your branding.
3. Simple Route:
Guests ought to have the option to find what they're searching for rapidly. Utilize a straightforward menu structure and instinctive design to conduct customers to key segments of your website.
4. Contact Information:
Make it simple for customers to contact you by conspicuously showing your contact information. Incorporate a telephone number, email address, and contact structure. If you have an actual area, add your location and a guide.
5. Clear Calls to take action (CTAs):
Urge guests to make explicit moves, for example, "Shop Currently," "Pursue Updates," or "Reach Us Today." Guarantee your CTAs stand apart with intense fastens and activity-arranged language.
6. Quick Burden Times:
A sluggish stacking website can drive guests away. Improve your website's presentation to guarantee pages' load in no less than three seconds or less.
7. Security Highlights:
Safeguard your customers' information by utilizing an SSL endorsement (search for the latch symbol in the program). This is particularly significant for internet business websites.

Tips for Easy to understand Design and Route

Your website ought to give a consistent and charming experience for guests. An easy-to-use configuration guarantees that guests stay longer, connect more and are bound to change over into customers.

Design Tips for Better Convenience:
1. Keep It Straightforward:
Stay away from the mess. Utilize void area really to make your content simple to peruse and explore.
2. Responsive Design:
Guarantee your website looks and works well on all gadgets, from work areas to cell phones. Use instruments like Google's Active Test to really look at your website's similarity.
3. Meaningful Textual styles:
Pick perfect, readable text styles. Keep away from excessively enlivening typefaces, and keep a predictable text dimension and style across your website.
4. Top notch Pictures:
Utilize proficient, high-goal pictures that line up with your brand. Keep away from nonexclusive stock photographs that can cause your website to feel indifferent.
5. Reliable Design:
Utilize a standard format across all pages to make a strong encounter. Guests ought to continuously know where to track down your menu, CTAs, and contact information.

Route Best Practices:

1. Sensible Menu Construction:
Coordinate your menu into clear classifications. For instance, an Internet business internet website could incorporate areas like "Shop," "About Us," "Blog," and "Contact."
2. Inward Engaging:
Guide guests to different pages on your website by including inward connections. For example, a blog entry could connection to a connected item or administration page.
3. Breadcrumbs:
Add breadcrumb route to assist customers with figuring out their area on your website and effectively return to past pages.

Improving FOR Mobile and Search Engines
In the present digital scene, a versatile and search-enhanced website is as of now not discretionary — it's fundamental.

Mobile Improvement Tips:
1. Focus on Speed:

Mobile customers expect quick burden times. Pack pictures and limit code to further develop performance.

2. Work on Route:
Utilize a burger menu for the mobile route, and guarantee fastens and interfaces are not difficult to tap with a finger.

3. Test Across Gadgets:
Consistently test your website on different cell phones and tablets to recognize and fix any issues.

Search engine optimization (SEO) Rudiments:
1. Utilize Significant Keywords:
Integrate keywords that your ideal interest group is probably going to look for into your headings, meta portrayals, and page content. Instruments like Google Catchphrase Organizer can assist with recognizing well-known terms.

2. Make Quality Content:
Internet crawlers focus on destinations with significant, unique content. Routinely update your internet website with blog entries, item portrayals, and FAQs that address customer needs.

3. Enhance Pictures and Videos:
Utilize distinct record names and alt text for pictures. Pack media records to lessen load times.

4. Assemble Backlinks:
Urge respectable websites to connect to your content. Backlinks sign to search engines that your internet page is reliable and pertinent.

5. Local SEO:
If your business serves a local audience, remember your city or locale for your keywords. Guarantee and enhance your Google My Business profile to further develop local pursuit visibility.

A viable website is something other than a digital presence — it's an instrument to draw in, connect with, and convert customers. By zeroing in on a proficient design, easy-to-use route, and mobile and Internet website design enhancement improvement, you'll make an Internet page that addresses your brand as well as drives significant outcomes for your business.

Your website is the groundwork of your internet marketing endeavors. With this setup, you're prepared to investigate strategies to draw in guests and transform them into faithful customers, which we'll cover in the accompanying sections.

CHAPTER 6: LEVERAGING LOCAL SEO

For small businesses, the force of local hunting couldn't possibly be more significant. At the point when potential customers look for services or items close to them, appearing in those indexed lists can fundamentally affect your business' visibility and development. Utilizing Local Search engine optimization guarantees that your business shows up unmistakably when close-by customers search for what you offer, driving people strolling through, inquiries, and Sales.

This part jumps into the significance of the local Search for small businesses, how to advance your Google My Business profile, and strategies for building local references and reviews.

Significance of Local Search for Small Companies

Local Search engine optimization centers around working on your business' visibility in area-based list items. For instance, when somebody looks for "best bistro close to me" or "handyman in Dallas," local Search engine optimization figures out which businesses appear.

Why Local SEO Matters:
1. Expanded Visibility:
Local Search engine optimization puts your business before expected customers at the specific second they are searching for your services or items.
2. High Change Rates:
Individuals looking locally are in many cases prepared to make a move — whether it's meeting your store, making a buy, or reaching you for help.
3. Mobile Use:
With the ascent of cell phones, local businesses have soared. As per Google, 76% of individuals who lead a local search visit a business in 24 hours or less.
4. Upper hand:
Small businesses can rival bigger businesses by overwhelming local list items. Local Search engine optimization evens the odds by focusing on customers in your local region.

Instructions to Enhance Google My Business

Google My Business (GMB), presently known as Google Business Profile, is one of the most incredible assets for local Internet optimization. This free platform permits you to deal with your business' online presence on Google Search and Guides.

Moves toward Streamline Your Google My Business Profile:
1. Guarantee and Confirm Your Profile:
In the event that you haven't as of now, guarantee your business on Google. Check is pivotal to guarantee that your information shows up in list items.
2. Give Total Information:

Finish up each segment of your profile, including your business name, address, telephone number (Rest), website, and business hours. Consistency across all platforms is critical.

3. Pick Precise Classifications:
Select essential and optional classifications that best depict your business. These classes assist Google with understanding your services and coordinate you with pertinent hunts.

4. Compose a Drawing in Depiction:
Highlight what makes your business extraordinary. Use keywords normally, yet center around making a portrayal that appeals to your ideal interest group.

5. Add Photographs and Videos:
Incorporate great pictures of your retail facade, items, group, or services. Visual content builds commitment and trust.

6. Empower Informing:
Initiate the informing element to permit customers to reach you straightforwardly from your profile. Answer instantly to inquiries to build trust.

7. Update Routinely:
Stay up with the latest changes in hours, new services, or advancements. Normal updates sign to research and customers that your business is active.

Building Local References and Reviews

Local references and reviews assume an imperative part in helping your local pursuit positioning and building validity. References allude to any specific of your business on the internet, while reviews furnish social verification that forms entrust with likely customers.

Local References:
1. Guarantee Consistency:
Your Rest information ought to be indistinguishable across all internet-based platforms, including catalogs, social media profiles, and your website. Conflicting information can confound internet search tools and hurt your rankings.

2. List Your Business in Online Catalogs:
Present your business to trustworthy catalogs like Howl, Business Conductor, and industry-explicit platforms. These references sign to search engines that your business is authentic and important.

3. Leverage Local Platforms:
Search for local indexes or local area websites where your business can be recorded. Being highlighted on platforms that take care of your area can essentially work on local visibility.

4. Use Construction Markup:
Add organized information to your website to assist with looking through motors to better figure out your business. Mapping markup works on your prospects showing up in rich query items.

Reviews:
1. Urge Fulfilled Customers to Leave Reviews:

Courteously demand reviews from cheerful customers through follow-up emails, instant emails, or in-person cooperation's.

2. Answer Reviews:

Thank customers for positive input and address any regrettable reviews professionally. Speedy, smart reactions show that you esteem customer input and are focused on progress.

3. Highlight Reviews on Your Website:

Show testimonials on your website to build trust and exhibit your brilliant assistance. Use instruments like gadgets or modules to pull reviews from Google or Howl.

4. Monitor Your Reputation:

Use apparatuses like Google Alarms or devoted standing administration programming to follow notices of your business on the internet. Address any issues speedily to keep a positive picture.

Local Internet optimization is a fundamental technique for small businesses hoping to draw in customers in their local region. By upgrading your Google My Business profile, guaranteeing reliable local references, and effectively managing customer reviews, you can fundamentally improve your visibility and validity.

With a solid local Internet optimization establishment, your business is better situated to flourish in a cutthroat market. In the following sections, we'll investigate extra systems to conduct people to your website and transform guests into faithful customers.

Part 3: Driving Traffic to Your Internet Website

CHAPTER 7: CONTENT MARKETING BASICS

In the digital age, content marketing has arisen as a foundation of effective online techniques. By creating and sharing valuable and meaningful content, small companies can draw in and connect with their ideal interest group, eventually driving customer activities that lead to development. This part investigates the force of content marketing, gives noteworthy platforms for making various types of content, and offers experiences in reusing content to amplify its range and viability.

The Power of Valuable Content in Drawing Customers

Content marketing goes past offering — it's tied in with conveying worth to your audience. Not at all like conventional publicizing, which hinders possible customers, content marketing draws in them by tending to their requirements, responding to their inquiries, and tackling their concerns.

Key Advantages of Content Marketing:
1. Builds Trust and Validity:
Routinely distributing supportive content positions your business as a professional in your industry. At the point when customers trust your aptitude, they're bound to pick your items or services.
2. Further develops Search Engine Optimization:
Top-notch content streamlined with important keywords further develops your website's internet search tool rankings, making it more straightforward for customers to track down you.
3. Creates Leads:
Content that reverberates with your audience urges them to make a move, for example, buying into your bulletin, downloading an aide, or reaching your business.
4. Connects with Your Audience:
Drawing in happy keeps your audience associated with your brand, cultivating faithfulness and long-term connections.
5. Financially cost-effective Marketing:
Content marketing frequently requires less business than customary publicizing while at the same time conveying long-term benefits, as great content keeps on drawing in customers after some time.

Making Websites, Videos, and Infographics

To prevail in happy marketing, center around making assorted types of content that take care of various inclinations and platforms.

Internet journals:
Blog entries remain one of the best-satisfied marketing apparatuses. They give top-to-bottom information on themes that make a difference to your audience and are perfect for supporting Internet optimization.

Pick Relevant Subjects:
Address normal inquiries or difficulties faced by your audience. Use instruments like Google Patterns or Answer General Society to recognize well-known search terms.

Utilize a Clear Structure:
Break your blog into segments with headings and subheadings for simple lucidness. Hold back nothing, proficient composition.

Incorporate a Call-to-Action (CTA):
Urge users to make the following stride, for example, pursuing your pamphlet or analyzing your services.

Videos:
Video content is exceptionally captivating and flexible, making it a fundamental piece of a small company's content procedure.

Types of Videos to Make:
Instructional exercises, item exhibitions, testimonials, in-the-background looks, or instructive content.

Keep It Brief:
Abilities to focus are short, so go for the gold two minutes except if the point requires more profundity.

Improve for Search engine optimization:
Add applicable keywords to your video title, depiction, and labels to further develop visibility on platforms like YouTube.

Infographics:
Infographics consolidate visuals and emails to introduce information in an effectively edible arrangement. They're ideal for summing up information, cycles, or correlations.

Design with Clarity:
Utilize basic visuals, clear textual styles, and predictable tones that line up with your brand.

Share Across Platforms:
Infographics perform well via social media and can conduct people to your website when shared in a calculated way.

Tips for Reusing Content Across Platforms

Making excellent content demands investment and assets. Reusing guarantees you get the most extreme worth from your endeavors by adjusting the content for different arrangements and platforms.

Strategies for Reusing Content:
1. Transform Blog Entries into Videos:
Utilize your blog's central issues to make a video script. Share the video on social media or embed it in your first blog post.
2. Make Infographics from Information Driven Posts:
If you've composed a blog with measurements or bit-by-bit processes, change the information into an infographic for fast visual utilization.
3. Separate Statements for Social media:
Pull key experiences or statements from your content and offer them as small posts on platforms like Instagram or LinkedIn.
4. Consolidate Content into Digital books or Guides:
Bunch-related blog entries or articles into a far-reaching guide that can be presented as a free download to create leads.
5. Have Online classes or Live Interactive Discussions:
Utilize your content as an establishment for intuitive meetings, permitting your audience to draw in with your brand continuously.
6. Update and Reuse Evergreen Content:
Invigorate more established users satisfied with new information or viewpoints and yet again share it to contact another audience or draw in existing devotees.

Content marketing is a strong, practical technique for small businesses to draw in, connect with, and convert customers. By zeroing in on significant internet websites, drawing in videos, and outwardly engaging infographics, you can give your audience the information they need in the organization they like. Reusing your content across numerous platforms augments its effect, guaranteeing that your endeavors drive reliable outcomes after some time.

CHAPTER 8: SOCIAL MEDIA MARKETING

Social media has changed how businesses communicate with their customers. For entrepreneurs, social media offers a strong, practical platform to construct brand awareness, draw in customers, and drive Sales. This part centers around how to pick the right social media platforms, make drawing in satisfied, and leverage paid to publicize to grow your compass and augment your marketing endeavors.

Picking The Right Platforms for Your Business

Not all social media platforms are made equivalent, and your business needn't bother to be on every one of them. Choosing the right platforms guarantees that your time and assets are spent really, interfacing with the audience probably going to draw in with your brand.

Understanding Platform Socioeconomics
1. Facebook:
With over 2.9 billion month-to-month active customers, Facebook appeals to a wide segment, making it ideal for businesses focusing on a different audience. It's especially successful for local businesses and those designing to construct local area commitment.
2. Instagram:
An outwardly determined platform with a more youthful segment, Instagram is ideally suited for businesses in businesses like style, food, travel, and wellness. Highlights like Stories and Reels permit inventive narrating and brand displaying.
3. LinkedIn:
LinkedIn takes care of professionals and B2B businesses. It's an extraordinary platform for sharing industry experiences, systems administration, and situating your brand as an idea chief.
4. Twitter:
Known for its speedy updates, Twitter functions admirably for businesses that need to share news, refresh, or take part in moving discussions.
5. TikTok:
This platform is quickly acquiring prominence among more youthful audiences. Businesses with an inventive edge can involve TikTok for short, captivating video content that grandstands items or recounts convincing stories.

Tips for Platform Choice

Understand where Your Listeners might be coming from: Pick platforms where your ideal interest group is generally active.
-Review Content Fit: Consider whether the platform upholds the sort of happy you intend to make.
-Begin Little: Spotlight on dominating a couple of platforms prior to extending to other people.

Strategies for Making Engaging Content
Whenever you've picked the right platforms, the following platform is to make content that catches consideration, energizes communication, and constructs an association with your audience.

1. Figure out Your Audience's interests
-Gather information to realize what content reverberates with your audience.
-Monitor commitment measurements like likes, remarks, and offers to distinguish famous posts.

2. Diversify Your Content
-Instructive Posts: Offer tips, how-to, and industry bits of knowledge.
-Engaging Content: Use humor, brands, or appealing stories to cultivate commitment.
-In the background: Grandstand the human side of your business with group presentations, office visits, or item creation processes.
-Customer Created Content: Urge customers to share photographs or testimonials including your items or services.

3. Use Visuals Effectively
Utilize great pictures and videos to catch consideration.
-Integrate marked illustrations or liveliness to make your posts stick out.
-Explore different avenues regarding live videos or Stories for ongoing commitment.

4. Keep up with Consistency
-Present routinely to keep your audience locked in.
-Foster a content schedule to design posts around occasions, occasions, and campaigns.

Running Paid Promotions to Extend Reach
Organic reach via social media can be restricted, particularly for new or small businesses. Paid publicizing permits you to contact a bigger audience, target explicit socioeconomics, and accomplish quantifiable outcomes.

Advantages of Social Media Publicizing
1. Exact Targeting:
Platforms like Facebook and Instagram permit you to target promotions in light old enough, area, interests, ways of behaving, and the sky is the limit from there.
2. Cost-effective Choices:
Little budgets can in any case yield critical outcomes, as most platforms offer adaptable evaluating models.
3. Speedy Outcomes:
Not at all like natural endeavors, paid advertisements can create prompt traffic and leads.

Types of Social Media Promotions
1. Supported Posts: Lift existing presents on increment visibility among your adherents and then some.
2. Merry go round Promotions: Exhibit different items or elements in a solitary advertisement.
3. Video Promotions: Utilize short, captivating videos to recount your brand story or highlight an item.
4. Lead Generation Promotions: Gather customer information straightforwardly through the platform with structures incorporated into the advertisement.

Making an Effective Ads Campaigns
-Define Clear Objectives: Know whether your promotion is pointed toward driving traffic, creating leads, or expanding Sales.
-Create Convincing Visuals and Copy: Use eye-catching visuals and brief, influential text.
-Incorporate Areas of strength for a to-Activity (CTA): Urge customers to make the ideal move, for example, "Shop Presently," "Find out More," or "Sign Up."
-Test and Enhance: Run A/B tests with various promotion varieties to distinguish what works best.

Measuring Promotion Performance
-Use platform analysis to follow measurements like active visitor clicking percentage (CTR), impressions, and transformation rates.
-Change focusing on, visuals, or copies given performance information to further develop results.

Social media marketing is an active, steadily developing scene that offers unmatched opportunities for private businesses to interface with their audience and drive development. By choosing the right platforms, creating engaging content, and using paid promotions, you can build a strong social media presence that enhances your overall marketing strategy.

CHAPTER 9: SEARCH ENGINE MARKETING (SEM)

Search Engine Marketing (SEM) furnishes entrepreneurs with a useful asset to increment visibility and draw in possible customers. Dissimilar to natural techniques that expect time to build up forward movement, SEM uses paid strategies like Google Advertisements to convey quick outcomes. This part investigates the basics of paid search, making powerful promotion campaigns, and measuring the profit from investment (return for capital invested) for your SEM endeavors.

Introduction to Paid Search

Paid search includes advancing your business through search engine publicizing platforms, fundamentally Google Advertisements and Bing Promotions. These platforms permit businesses to offer keywords applicable to their items or services. At the point when customers look for those terms, your promotions show up at the highest point of the query items, conducting people to your website.

Why Paid Search Matters
1. Prompt Visibility: Not at all like natural strategies that require some investment to rank, SEM places your business before potential customers right away.
2. Profoundly Designated: Paid search guarantees your promotions are seen by individuals effectively looking for items or services you offer.
3. Adaptable: SEM budgets can be custom-fitted to businesses of any size, making it open to entrepreneurs.

Key Platforms for Paid Search
1. Google Advertisements: The most famous platform, with admittance to billions of day-to-day looks. It offers a broad focus on choices and devices for crusading the board.
2. Bing Promotions: However more modest in reach, Bing Advertisements can be more cost-effective because of lower rivalry.

Instructions to Make Viable Promotion Campaigns
The progress of an SEM technique depends on all-around arranged and executed crusades.
1. Defining Campaign Targets
-Each SEM mission ought to have an unmistakable objective, whether it's driving website traffic, producing leads, or expanding Sales.
-Traffic Objectives: Spotlight on keywords with high inquiry volumes.
-Lead Generation Objectives: Use landing pages intended for catching contact information.
-Sales Objectives: Incorporate solid suggestions to take action (CTAs) like "Purchase Now" or "Get a Free Statement."

2. Conducting Keyword Exploration

Choosing the right keywords is basic for arriving at your main interest group.
-Use Keyword Instruments: Platforms like Google Catchphrase Organizer and SEMrush assist with distinguishing high-performing keywords.
-Center around Lengthy Tail Keywords: Expressions like "reasonable internet website architecture for small businesses " are not so much serious but rather more prone to change over.
-Negative Keywords: Reject unimportant terms to try not to squander promotion spend. For instance, in the event that you're a superior help, you might reject keywords like "modest" or "free."

3. Composing Convincing Promotion Copy
-Your promotion copy is the initial feeling potential customers have of your business.
-Title: Catch consideration with clear, benefit-driven information.
-Portrayal: Highlight extraordinary selling focuses (USPs) and incorporate a CTA.
-Show URL: Guarantee the URL mirrors the promotion's content to assemble trust.

Example:
Title: "Reasonable Internet website architecture for Small Companies"
Portrayal: "Custom websites beginning at $499. Quick circle back. Help your online presence today!"
CTA: "Get a Free Statement Now!"

4. Setting a Fitting Budget
-Day to day Budget: Conclude the amount you're willing to go through every day to abstain from overspending.
-Bid Strategy: Pick between manual offering (you set the greatest bid per click) or mechanized offering (the platform improves offers for you).

Measuring Return for Money Invested from Your SEM Endeavors

Following and analyzing the exhibition of your SEM crusades guarantees you capitalize on your business.

1. Key Measurements to Monitor
-Active clicking factor (CTR): The level of customers who click on your promotion. High CTRs show successful promotion copy and focusing on.
-Cost-Per-Snap (CPC): The typical expense of each snap on your promotion. Lower CPCs assist with boosting your budget.
-Change Rate: The level of customers who make an ideal move, like making a buy or pursuing a pamphlet.
-Quality Score: Google's evaluating of your promotion's importance to the objective catchphrase. Higher scores bring about lower expenses and better position.

2. Utilizing Analytics Devices
-Google Promotions Dashboard: Gives point by point bits of knowledge into crusade performance, including impressions, clicks, and changes.
-Google Analysis: Coordinates with Google Promotions to follow customer conduct on your website subsequent to clicking a promotion.

3. Changing Campaigns for Improved Results
-A/B Testing: Trial with various promotion copies, CTAs, or landing pages to distinguish what reverberates most with your audience.
-Streamline Keywords: Interrupt low-performing keywords and apportion more budget to high-changing ones.
-Further develop Landing pages: Guarantee pages are quick stacking, versatile, and lined up with promotional content.

Tips for Long-term Success with SEM
SEM is certainly not a limited-time offer technique — it requires continuous streamlining and transformation to remain cutthroat.

Remain Updated on Trends
Search engine calculations and promotion platforms highlight advances continually. Remain informed through industry online journals, online courses, and updates from platforms like Google Advertisements.

Consolidate SEM with Search Engine Optimization
While SEM offers prompt outcomes, consolidating it with Search engine optimization (Search engine optimization) guarantees practical, long-term development. Use bits of knowledge from your paid campaigns to illuminate your natural strategies.

Center around Customer Experience
Promotions might drive traffic, however, a positive website experience guarantees changes. Put resources into quick stacking pages, instinctive routes, and clear CTAs to take advantage of your SEM endeavors.

Search Engine Marketing is a vital device for private businesses looking for speedy visibility and quantifiable outcomes. Via cautiously arranging efforts, picking the right keywords, and following performance measurements, you can guarantee that your interest in SEM conveys serious areas of strength for a strong return.

CHAPTER 10: EMAIL MARKETING FOR SMALL BUSINESSES

Email marketing is a foundation of digital marketing for small businesses. It offers an immediate, individual method for drawing in with your audience, constructing connections, and driving Sales. With the right systems, you can develop your email list, make drawing-in emails, and mechanize campaigns to save time while boosting leverage.

Building and Developing Your Email List
An email list is the underpinning of your email marketing endeavors. A well-organized list guarantees that your emails arrive intrigued and connected with beneficiaries.

1. Offer Worth in Return for Emails
Individuals are bound to share their contact information when they see esteem in doing so. Instances of captivating offers include:
-Rebate Codes: "Join and get 10% off your most memorable buy."
-Selective Content: digital books, guides, or admittance to online courses custom-made to your audience's necessities.
-Free Preliminaries or Tests: Especially compelling for item-based businesses.

2. Set out Simple Information Exchange Opportunities
Simplify it for possible customers to join your email list by:
-Inserting Information Exchange Structures: Remember structures for your landing page, blog entries, and contact pages.
-Utilizing Popups Decisively: Coordinated popups or leave goal popups urge guests to buy in without being meddling.
-Utilizing Social Media: Advance your email information exchange structure on platforms like Facebook, Instagram, and LinkedIn.

3. Guarantee Consistence with Email Regulations
Comply with guidelines like the CAN-SPAM Act by:
-Giving a reasonable selection in the process.
-Counting a withdrawal connection in each email.
-Involving a substantial actual location in your email footer.

Composing Engaging Email that Convert
Creating convincing Emails is a workmanship. Each email ought to convey esteem while prodding beneficiaries toward making a move.

1. Begin with Serious areas of strength for a Line
The headline decides if your email is opened or disregarded. Successful titles are:

-Concise: Aim for 6-10 words.
-Captivating: Arouse interest without turning to misleading content.
-Customized: Utilize the beneficiary's name or reference their inclinations.

Models:
-"Selective Deal Only for You!"
-"5 Hints to Lift Your Business Today."

2. Center around Clear and Succinct Content
    Try not to overpower your audience with indulgent emails. All things considered:
-Highlight the Worth: Immediately make sense of what the user will acquire.
-Use List items: Separate information for simple lucidness.
-End with a Source of inspiration (CTA): Guide users on what to do straightaway, like visiting your website or making a buy.

3. Add Visual Appeal
    Visuals make your emails captivating and significant. Include:
-Branding Components: Reliable utilization of your logo, tones, and text styles.
-Pictures or GIFs: Applicable visuals that optimize the message.
-Whitespace: Stay away from mess to keep up with lucidness.

Automating Efforts TO Save Time
    Email computerization permits you to sustain leads and draw in customers without consistent manual exertion.

1. Welcome Emails
Welcome emails are your most memorable opportunity to establish areas of strength for a.
-Send following somebody buys in.
-Present your business, highlight key contributions, and set assumptions for future emails.

Example:
Subject: "Welcome to [Your Business Name]!"
Body: "We're excited to have you here. Here is an extraordinary 15% markdown on your most memorable buy."

2. Dribble Campaigns
    Dribble crusades convey a progression of emails over the long run, conducting supporters through a journey.
-Instructive Series: Give tips or bits of knowledge connected with your items or services.
-Special Series: Highlight occasional offers or restricted time bargains.

3. Truck Surrender Emails
   For internet based business businesses, truck relinquishment emails recuperate likely lost Sales.
-Help customers to remember the things left in their truck.
-Offer an impetus, like free delivery or a rebate, to support culmination.

4. Re-Commitment Campaigns
   Keep your email list now by re-engaging dormant supporters.
-Inquire as to whether they're inspired by your content.
-Give a convincing motivation to remain, like elite updates or offers.

Measuring The Outcome of Your Email Marketing
Consistently analyzing email performance assists you with refining your technique and accomplishing improved results.

1. Key Measurements to Track
   Open Rate: Shows the level of beneficiaries who open your email. Work on this by testing titles and sending times.
-Active visitor clicking percentage (CTR): Measures the number of beneficiaries that snap on joins inside your email.
-Change Rate: Tracks the number of beneficiaries that total an ideal activity, like making a buy or pursuing help.
-Withdraw Rate: A high rate could flag unimportant content or too-regular emails.

2. A/B Testing
    Explore different avenues regarding various components of your emails to figure out what reverberates best with your audience. Test:

-Titles.
-Email length and construction.
-Kinds of CTAs.

3. Optimize for Mobile
With most emails being opened on cell phones, guarantee your emails:
+Utilize responsive design.
-Highlight succinct headlines and pre-headers.
-Keep away from enormous pictures or minuscule text styles.

Tips for Long-Term Success with Email Marketing

Consistency and pertinence are critical to keeping areas of strength for a marketing technique.

1. Keep an Ordinary Timetable
Lay out a steady email rhythm to keep your audience locked in. For instance, send a week-after-week pamphlet or month-to-month item refreshes.

2. Portion Your Audience
Partition your email list into sections given elements like socioeconomics, buy history, or interests. This guarantees your content applies to each gathering.

Example: Send selective proposals to visit buyers while offering instructive content to new endorsers.

3. Customize Whenever the situation allows
Use email marketing programming to customize emails with the beneficiary's name, late buys, or perusing history. Customized emails increment commitment and encourage dedication.

Email marketing offers small businesses an unmatched chance to interface with customers and drive Sales. By developing your list, creating connections with emails, and utilizing computerization, you can construct a feasible and effective marketing system.

Part 4: Converting Visitors into Customers

CHAPTER 11: OPTIMIZING YOUR SALES FUNNEL

A very well-designed Sales pipe is fundamental for conducting possible customers from introductory attention to making a buy. For entrepreneurs, streamlining this journey guarantees that each collaboration with an imminent customer is significant and effective. By understanding the phases of the buyer's journey, sustaining leads successfully, and using devices to follow performance, you can make a consistent way that transforms interest into Sales.

Understanding the Phases of the Buyer's Journey
The Sales pipe is separated into particular platforms, each requiring fitted systems to keep prospects connected with and advancing toward transformation.

1. Awareness
The awareness stage is where potential customers first experience your brand.
-Objective: Catch consideration and lay out your business as an answer to their concern.

Strategies:
-Make educational blog entries, videos, or social media content.
-Utilize designated promotions to contact your optimal audience.

Leverage Internet optimization to rank for important keywords.
-Example: A little bread kitchen could distribute a blog named, "10 Ways to pick the Ideal Birthday Cake," situating itself as a specialist in the field.

2. Thought
In this stage, prospects are assessing their choices.
-Objective: Exhibit the interesting worth of your items or services.

Strategies:
-Share customer testimonials and contextual analyses.
-Give point by point item information and analysis.
-Offer free assets, like aides or preliminaries.
-Example: An internet based wellness mentor could offer a free 7-day exercise intend to exhibit their mastery and energize recruits.

3. Choice
At this stage, prospects are prepared to pursue a buy choice.

-Objective: Give the last push to change over leads into customers.

Strategies:
-Offer restricted time discounts or advancements.
-Utilize clear and convincing invitations to take action (CTAs).
-Guarantee a frictionless buying process.
-Example: A dress shop could send an email with a 15% markdown code and an immediate connection to the checkout page.

Step-by-step Instructions to Support Leads and Empower Conversions

Compelling lead sustaining keeps your prospects drew in and assembles trust after some time.

1. Use Email Marketing Efforts
-Email stays one of the best instruments for sustaining leads.
-Send welcome emails presenting your brand and incentive.
-Share instructive content to address problem areas.
-Offer selective arrangements to support changes.
-Example: A skincare brand could send an email succession making sense of the advantages of its items, matched with customer testimonials and a markdown offer.

2. Customize the Customer Experience
-Fitting your collaborations to individual inclinations optimizes commitment.
-Use information from website visits, email clicks, or past buys to illuminate your informing.
-Section your audience in light of interests, socioeconomics, or conduct.
-Example: A pet stock store could send customized proposals given the kind of pet a customer possesses.

3. Leverage Retargeting Advertisements
Retargeting advertisements remind likely customers about your business after they've collaborated with your website or items.
-Show advertisements highlighting things they saw yet didn't buy.
-Highlight positive reviews or proposition a rebate code.
-Example: A home style store could show retargeting promotions highlighting a seat that a guest left in their truck.

Devices to Track and Further Develop Channel Performance

Following the presentation of your Sales channel permits you to recognize bottlenecks and make informed changes.

1. Use Analytics Platforms
Platforms like Google Analysis, HubSpot, or CRM apparatuses give important bits of knowledge.

-Monitor website traffic and customer conduct.
-Track change rates at each pipe platform.
-Recognize drop-off focuses and advance them.
-Example: Assuming information shows numerous customers leave your website at the checkout page, consider improving on the interaction or offering free delivery.

2. Set Up Key Performance Indicators (KPIs)
-KPIs assist you with measuring the viability of your channel. Key measurements include:
-Cost Per Lead (CPL): The amount you spend to obtain each lead.
-Customer Obtaining Cost (CAC): The expense of changing over a lead into a paying customer.
-Lifetime Worth (LTV): The complete income a customer creates during their relationship with your business.

3. Conduct A/B Testing
-Testing various components of your channel can uncover what works best.
-Test varieties of CTAs, landing pages, or email headlines.
-Use bits of knowledge to carry out changes that drive improved results.
-Example: A internet based business internet page could test two forms of an item page — one with a "Purchase Presently" button and one more with a "Find out More" button — to see which prompts more transformations.

Ways to Advance Each Channel Platforms

Each phase of the channel requires consistent refinement to accomplish the most extreme outcomes.

1. Awareness Stage Improvement
-Center around top-notch content that resounds with your main interest group.
-Team up with leverages or accomplices to extend your span.
2. Thought Stage Enhancement
-Give inside and out assets like contextual analysis, video demos, or online courses.
-Address normal complaints or worries through FAQs and backing.
3. Choice Stage Streamlining
Improve on the checkout cycle with insignificant advances and different installment choices. Use criticalness and shortage strategies, similar to commencement clocks or restricted stock warnings, to energize quick activity.

Upgrading your Sales channel guarantees a smooth and compensating customer business. By seeing each platform, supporting leads successfully, and utilizing information to refine your strategy, you can augment changes and develop your business economically.

CHAPTER 12: CRAFTING HIGH-CONVERTING LANDING PAGES

A landing page fills in as the initial feeling for likely customers and assumes a crucial part in your digital marketing strategy. Dissimilar to general internet website pages, landing pages are custom-made to drive explicit activities, like buying an item, pursuing a bulletin, or downloading an asset. By understanding the fundamental parts of an effective landing page, making convincing copies, and constantly testing performance, entrepreneurs can essentially increment changes and accomplish their marketing objectives.

Components of an Effective Landing Page
 A compelling landing page is a blend of key design, influential content, and customer-driven usefulness. Every component adds to conducting guests toward making the ideal move.
1. Clear and Engaging with Title
-Your title is the primary thing guests see and should catch consideration right away.
-Utilize compact language to convey esteem.
-Center around tackling an issue or tending to a need.
-Example: Rather than "Welcome to Our Website," use "Lift Your Efficiency with Our Basic Devices."

2. Solid Visuals
-Top-notch pictures or videos optimize the allure of your landing page.
-Exhibit your item or administration in real life.
-Guarantee visuals are important and proficient.
-Example: A wellness application could utilize a brief video showing its elements.

3. Centered Call-to Action (CTA)
-A reasonable and convincing CTA guides customers to make the following stride.
-Use activity-situated language, for example, "Begin Now" or "Guarantee Your Markdown."
-Position the CTA noticeably on the page.

4. Trust-Building Components
-Laying out trust is pivotal to changing over guests.
-Incorporate testimonials, reviews, or contextual analysis.
-Show logos of accomplices, confirmations, or grants.
-Example: A home cleaning administration could highlight positive customer reviews alongside a fulfillment ensure identification.

5. Minimal Interruptions
-A landing page ought to have a solitary concentration to try not to befuddle guests.
-Eliminate route menus or inconsequential connections.

-Keep the format perfect and cleaned up.
-Example: A page advancing a digital book download ought to zero in exclusively on the book's worth and advantages, without any connects to different pages.

Composing Convincing Copy and CTAS

Words hold the ability to convince. Creating powerful copy and CTAs can have the effect between a skip and a change.

1. Speak Straightforwardly to Your Audience
-Address the user's necessities and desires.
-Utilize conversational language to make an association.
-Highlight how your proposition takes care of their concern or optimizes their life.
-Example: "Battling to remain coordinated? Find the organizer that makes using time effectively easy!"

2. Stress Advantages Over Elements
-While highlights are significant, benefits resound more with your audience.
-Make sense of how your item or administration works on the customer's insight.
-Use list items to introduce key advantages.
-Example: Rather than "Our product incorporates 10 modules," state "Professional your funds with instruments that streamline designing and following."

3. Create Urgency
-Energize prompt activity by presenting a need to get going.
-Use phrases like "Restricted Time Offer" or "Just 5 Spots Left."
-Highlight cutoff times or restrictive arrangements.
-Example: "Join before noon to save 20% on your membership!"

4. Optimize the CTA
-The CTA ought to be activity arranged, apparent, and lined up with the page's objective.
-Utilize differentiating varieties to make the CTA stick out.
-Keep the text compact, with clear guidelines.
-Example: Rather than "Submit," use "Download My Free Aide Now."

Testing and Further Developing Page Performance

Indeed, even the most all around made landing pages' benefit from constant improvement. By analyzing performance and testing transforms, you can amplify their viability.

1. Monitor Key Measurements
-Use analysis devices to follow significant performance indicators, for example,

-Change Rate: The level of guests who complete the ideal activity.
-Bob Rate: The level of guests who leave without locking in.
-Time on Page: How long guests stay at your point of arrival.
-Example: Assuming your change rate is low, think about updating your CTA or improving on the structure.

2. Conduct A/B Testing
-A/B testing permits you to look at two forms of a landing page to see which performs better.
-Test varieties of titles, pictures, or CTAs.
-Execute changes in light of information-driven results.
-Example: A realtor could test one title that peruses "Find Your Fantasy Home Today" against another that says "Find Homes You'll Cherish."

3. Optimize for Speed and Mobile
-Page load time and mobile similarity fundamentally leverage customer experience.
-Guarantee your landing page stacks rapidly on all gadgets.
-Utilize responsive design to give a consistent versatile encounter.
-Example: Pack pictures and limit coding mistakes to decrease load times.

4. Assemble Customer Feedback
-Conduct feedback from customers can give important bits of knowledge.
-Use studies or heatmaps to recognize areas of disarray.
-Carry out ideas to further develop route and clearness.
-Example: Assuming customers report trouble finding the CTA button, reposition it for better visibility.

Methods for Creating Landing Pages that Convert
   By following prescribed strategies, you can make presentation pages that reliably convey results.

1. Focus Above the top Content
Guarantee basic information and CTAs are apparent without looking over them.
2. Adjust Landing pages to Promotion Campaigns
Keep up with consistency between your promotion copy and the landing page to build up your message.
3. Keep Structures Basic
Just ask fundamental information to diminish friction.
For example: For a bulletin information exchange, demand simply the email address as opposed to extra private subtleties.
4. Use Leave Purpose Popups

Catch customers who are going to leave with a last deal or update.
-Example: "Stand by! Try not to Botch Your Opportunity to Save 10% on Your Most Memorable Buy."

Making high-converting landing pages requires a mix of key design, powerful copy, and information driven enhancement. By zeroing in on the necessities of your audience and persistently refining your strategy, you can transform easygoing guests into steadfast customers.

CHAPTER 13: THE POWER OF ONLINE REVIEWS AND TESTIMONIALS

In the present digital scene, online reviews and testimonials are basic for building trust and believability with expected customers. They act as friendly evidence, impacting purchasing choices and offering consolation about the nature of your items or services. As an entrepreneur, utilizing internet feedback really can essentially support your brand's standing, draw in new customers, and further develop customer maintenance.

This section investigates strategies to empower positive reviews, handle negative input professionally, and show testimonials to boost their effect on your business achievement.

Empowering Fulfilled Customers to Leave Reviews

Customer reviews assume an urgent part in molding public discernment. Numerous customers will leave input whenever provoked, however, it's vital to simplify the interaction and fulfillment.

1. Ask Brilliantly
Timing is basic while mentioning reviews. The best minutes to ask include:
-After a successful collaboration, a customer praises your management either in person or via email.
-Upon item conveyance: Incorporate a note or follow-up email asking for feedback.
-In the wake of settling a customer issue: Fulfilled goals frequently lead to gleaming reviews.

2. Make it Simple
Diminish erosion by giving conduct connections to review platforms like Google, Howl, or Trustpilot.
-Add interactive connections in emails or instant emails.
-Use QR codes on receipts or item bundling to conduct customers straightforwardly to review pages.

3. Boost without Paying off
While offering limits or gifts in return for reviews is restricted on most platforms, you can energize cooperation by showing appreciation.
-Highlight how reviews help your business develop and further develop services.
-Send cards to say thanks to customers who leave feedback.

4. Leverage Email Follow-Up
Automated emails can provoke reviews.
-Incorporate customized emails saying thanks to customers for their buy.
-Tenderly solicitation feedback while underscoring the significance of their feedback.

-Example: "Your viewpoint matters! Kindly pause for a minute to share your experience and help other people find [Your Business Name]."

Managing Negative Feedback Professionally

No business is invulnerable to analysis, yet how you handle negative reviews can altogether mean for your standing. An insightful reaction can transform a disappointed customer into a dedicated backer.

1. Answer Instantly

Fast reactions show that you esteem customer input and are focused on settling issues.
-Recognize the objection and express sympathy.
-Stay away from delays, as quietness might seem pompous.
-Example: "We're sorry to learn about your experience and value you drawing this out into the open."

2. Keep it Proficient and Affable

Regardless of whether a review feels ridiculous, keep a well-mannered and deferential tone.
-Stay away from cautious or angry language.
-Center around getting it and resolving the issue.
-Example: "Thank you for your input. We seriously view your interests and might want to learn more to make things right."

3. Offer a Solution

Exhibit a readiness to determine the issue by offering significant arrangements.
-Give a discount, substitution, or future markdown if proper.
-Take the discussion disconnected to secretly talk about subtleties.
-Example: "If it's not too much trouble, get in touch with us at [email or telephone number] so we can determine this matter straightforwardly."

4. Learn and Improve

Utilize negative input as an amazing chance to distinguish regions for development.
-Break down repeating issues and carry out changes to forestall future issues.
-Show customers that their feedback drives enhancements.
-Example: After a few grumblings about transportation delays, think about changing your designed operations system.

Showing Testimonials to Lift Trust

Positive testimonials are a strong marketing device. When shown in an intelligent way, they can altogether impact potential customers' buying choices.

1. Highlight Testimonials on Your Website

Your website is an essential touchpoint for expected customers, making it the best area for displaying positive feedback.

-Add a devoted "Testimonials" or "Customer Reviews" page.
-Show statements on your landing page or item pages.
-Example: Remember a merry-go-round of testimonials for your landing page for high visibility.

2. Utilize Visual Format
Visual content, like videos or photographs, improves the validity of testimonials.
-Ask that customers give video reviews or pictures of them utilizing your item.
-Consolidate text reviews with star appraisals for added leverage.
-Example: A skincare brand could include when photographs put together by blissful customers.

3. Integrate Reviews into Marketing Materials
Testimonials can reinforce your marketing efforts across different channels.
-Use customer quotes in social media posts or email pamphlets.
-Add reviews to printed materials, like leaflets or flyers.
-Example: A social media posts with a shining customer review and an item picture can build trust and commitment.

4. Grandstand Assorted Input
Highlight testimonials from various kinds of customers to reverberate with a more extensive audience.
-Include reviews that underline different advantages of your item or administration.
-Guarantee credibility by showing genuine names and, whenever the situation allows, photographs.
-Example: A wellness mentor could incorporate testimonials from customers of various ages and wellness levels.

Utilizing On the internet Review Platforms

Outside platforms are fundamental for laying out validity past your website.

1. Enhance Your Profiles
Guarantee and complete profiles on well-known review locales like Google My Business, Cry, and Trustpilot.
-Incorporate modern contact information and business depictions.
-Transfer proficient photographs and logos.

2. Energize Cross-Platform Reviews
Ask that fulfilled customers leaves feedback on numerous platforms.
-Give connects to review pages in follow-up emails or on receipts.
-Monitor and answer reviews on all platforms to show commitment.

3. Track Your Online Reputation

Use apparatuses to monitor and investigate customer input across platforms.

-Recognize patterns in reviews to pinpoint qualities and shortcomings.

-Answer all reviews, showing appreciation for positive ones and tending to worries in bad ones.

The Effect of Reviews on Search Engine Optimization

Positive reviews construct trust as well as optimize your Internet website streamlining (Internet optimization).

1. Support Local Pursuit Visibility

-Google thinks about review amount, quality, and recency while positioning local businesses.

-Empower reviews on Google My Business to work on local rankings.

2. Increment Website Clicks

List items including high appraisals or positive bits draw in additional clicks.

-Answering reviews signals action and commitment to internet engines.

-Example: A 4.8-star normal rating on Google can make your business stand apart from contenders.

Online reviews and testimonials are significant resources for entrepreneurs. By effectively reassuring input, taking care of analysis effortlessly, and exhibiting positive testimonials, you can lay out trust, draw in new customers, and cultivate loyalty.

Part 5: Sustaining Long-term Success

CHAPTER 14: ANALYZING INFORMATION AND ADJUSTING STRATEGIES

In the present digital scene, information is the foundation of fruitful online strategies. Whether you're managing a personal blog, an online business platform, or a corporate website, tracking and analysis provide valuable insights into customer behavior, campaign performance, and overall business growth. Without a clear understanding of these metrics, even the best-laid strategies can struggle to succeed.

This part underscores the significance of information analysis, investigates apparatuses to quantify key measurements like website traffic and Sales, and talks about how to change campaigns to optimize results in light of information experiences.

The Significance of Tracking Analysis

Tracking analysis isn't just about gathering numbers; it's tied in with interpreting crude information into significant bits of knowledge. These experiences can highlight what's working, uncover failing to meet expectations regions, and give guidance for future endeavors.

1. Understanding Customer Conduct
Analysis shows how customers communicate with your website, from the pages they visit to the time they spend on unambiguous content. This information can uncover:
-Which pages draw in the most rush hour gridlock?
-The places where customers drop off or forsake their journey.
-How your website is engaging with its audience.

2. Upgrading Marketing Campaigns
By examining information from crusades, you can gauge key performance markers (KPIs) like navigate rates (CTR), transformation rates, and profit from investment (return on initial capital investment). This guarantees your marketing endeavors are financially cost-effective and effective.

3. Improving Decision Making
Information-driven systems eliminate mystery. The analysis permits you to back your choices with proof, lessening gambles and further developing results.

4. Distinguishing Patterns and Valuable opportunities

Observing information over the long run recognizes examples and patterns. For example, occasional spikes in rush hour gridlock or abrupt drops in commitment can determine when and how to send off crusades.

Tools to Measure Website Traffic, Commitment, and Sales

Different apparatuses are accessible to follow and break down website performance. Picking the right devices relies upon your particular objectives, whether you're hoping to understand customer commitment, monitor Sales, or measure marketing viability. The following are the absolute most dependable and generally utilized analysis devices:

1. Google Analysis
Google Analysis is an extensive device for following website traffic and customer conduct.

Key Highlights:
-Traffic sources: Comprehend where your guests come from (search engines, social media, conduct traffic).
-Customer socioeconomics: Gain bits of knowledge into age, orientation, and interests.
-Conduct stream: Perceive how customers explore your website.
-Transformation following: Measure objective fulfillments, for example, buys or recruits.
-Why Use It: It's free, strong, and incorporates flawlessly with other Google devices like Promotions and Search Control Center.

2. HOTJAR
Hotjar centers around customer association through heatmaps, meeting accounts, and feedback devices.

Key Highlights:
-Heatmaps: Imagine where customers snap, scroll, and float.
-Meeting accounts: Watch continuous customer meetings to recognize convenience issues.
-Reviews: Gather conduct input from guests.
-Why Use It: Ideal for further developing customer experience (UX) and recognizing trouble spots.

3. SEMRUSH
SEMrush spends significant time in Internet website optimization and contender analysis yet additionally offers traffic and commitment experiences.

Key Elements:
-Keyword following: Monitor your website's rankings for target keywords.
-Contender experiences: Contrast your traffic and strategies with contenders.
-Traffic analysis: Comprehend audience conduct and reference sources.

-Why Use It: Ideal for advancing internet search tool performance and remaining in front of contenders.

4. Shopify Analysis (for Internet business)
For online stores utilizing Shopify, this underlying analysis device gives Sales and customer experiences.

Key Highlights:
-Sales reports: Track income, top-selling items, and normal order esteem.
-Customer conduct: Investigate checkout cycles and truck deserting rates.
-Marketing reports: Measure the return on money invested in email campaigns and promotions.
-Why Use It: Custom fitted for internet business businesses to comprehend and further develop Sales performance.

5. Social media Analysis Instruments
Platforms like Facebook, Instagram, and LinkedIn offer inherent analysis for following commitment and reach. Outsider apparatuses like Hootsuite or Grow Social give cross-platform experiences.

Key Elements:
-Post-performance: Track likes, offers, and remarks.
-Audience development: Monitor supporter counts and commitment patterns.
-Crusade following Measure the outcome of paid promotions.
-Why Use It: Critical for businesses depending on social media to drive traffic and transformations.

Adjusting Campaigns Based on Data Insights
Information analysis is just significant on the off chance that it prompts activity. Whenever you've assembled information, the subsequent platform is to change your strategies to amplify leverage. This is the way to utilize analysis to refine your campaigns:

1. Recognize Points of concern
Begin by pinpointing failing to meet expectations regions in your campaigns or website.

Models:
-High bob rates might show superfluous content or slow-stacking pages.
-Low change rates could flag ineffectively designed landing pages or indistinct suggestions to take action (CTAs).
-Declining traffic might propose a requirement for refreshed content or further developed Internet website design enhancement.

2. A/B Testing for Improvement
A/B testing includes making two renditions of a page, email, or promotion to see which performs better.

Steps:
- Transform each factor in turn, for example, title text, button tones, or pictures.
- Use analysis apparatuses to follow performance measurements like CTR or transformation rates.
- Execute the triumphant adaptation and keep testing different components.

3. REFINE Focusing on AND Informing
- Analysis can uncover bits of knowledge about your audience's socioeconomics and inclinations. Utilize this information to tailor your informing and focusing on.

Changes:
- Center around platforms where your audience is generally active.
- Make content that lines up with customer interests or ways of behaving.
- Refine promotion focusing on arriving at the most drawn-in fragments of your audience.

4. Monitor AND SCALE Fruitful Techniques
At the point when campaigns perform well, recognize the variables adding to their prosperity and repeat these across different drives.

For example: If a social media post drives huge traffic, analyze its components — visuals, tone, timing — and apply comparative strategies to future posts.

5. Put forth Sensible Objectives AND BENCHMARKS
Analysis assists with laying out quantifiable objectives, guaranteeing your endeavors stay engaged and achievable.
- Cost-effective Objectives: Make objectives that are Explicit, Quantifiable, Reachable, Significant, and Time-bound.
- Benchmarks: Look at your information against industry principles or past performance to follow progress.

The Power of Ceaseless Improvement

Analyzing data and changing techniques is a continuous cycle, not a one-time task. The digital scene develops quickly, and remaining serious requires consistent transformation. By focusing on standard data analysis and key changes, you can guarantee:

Expanded return for money invested: Improved focusing on and advancement lead to better asset assignment.

Improved Customer Experience: Understanding and addressing customer needs encourages reliability and trust.

Supported Development: Information-driven choices make serious areas of strength for long-term achievement.

Information is the backbone of any fruitful internet-based strategy. By utilizing analysis devices and consistently refining your strategy in view of experiences, you can amplify commitment, drive changes, and accomplish your objectives.

CHAPTER 15: MANAGING YOUR MARKETING BUDGET

Effectively dealing with a marketing budget is the foundation of fruitful business development. Whether you're a small business with restricted assets or an enormous organization endeavoring to enhance spending, a very much-arranged budget guarantees each dollar adds to significant results. Without key distribution, businesses risk overspending on inadequate campaigns or passing up on chances to amplify returns.

This part centers around distributing assets for the most extreme effect, investigates minimal expense strategies custom-fitted for small businesses and highlights normal spending entanglements to keep away from.

Dispensing Assets for Greatest Effect

Marketing budgets ought to be decisively dispensed to regions that convey the best profit from investment (return for capital invested). To accomplish this, businesses need to adjust spending to their targets, track performance, and stay sufficiently adaptable to adjust when needs shift.

1. Put forth Clear Objectives

Begin by defining what you intend to accomplish through your marketing endeavors. Objectives might incorporate expanding website traffic, producing leads, supporting Sales, or further developing brand awareness. Having clear targets designates assets to drives that straightforwardly support those objectives.

2. Focus on High-Effect Channels

Not all marketing channels offer a similar worth. Center around platforms that convey quantifiable outcomes in light of your interest group and industry.
-Digital Publicizing: Paid promotions on platforms like Google and Facebook are exceptionally successful for contacting designated audiences.
-Content Marketing: Internet journals, videos, and social media posts assemble natural traffic over the long run.
-Email Marketing: A reasonable method for drawing in customers and support leads.

3. Partition the Budget in an intelligent way

Dispense your budget across three principal regions:
-Brand Awareness: Exercises like social media campaigns and content creation.
-Lead Age: Endeavors, for example, pay-per-click (PPC) publicizing and Internet optimization.
-Maintenance: Strategies like dedication programs and customized email campaigns to continue to keep customers locked in.

4. Monitor return for capital invested

Routinely track the exhibition of your campaigns to recognize regions conveying the best return on initial capital investment. Redistribute assets from failing to meet expectations exercises to those showing the most commitment.

5. Plan for Adaptability

Markets and patterns can change rapidly. Save a piece of your budget (5-10%) for trial campaigns or unforeseen opportunities that emerge.

Minimal expense Techniques for Small businesses

Small companies frequently work with restricted marketing budgets, yet asset requirements don't need to restrict inventiveness or viability. Here are a few financially cost-effective strategies that convey results without burning through every last cent.

1. Leverage Social media

Social media platforms like Instagram, Facebook, and TikTok offer free instruments to arrive at expected customers.
-Content Creation: Offer drawing in posts, stories, and videos that resonate with your audience.
-Local Area Commitment: Answer remarks and partake in discussions to build brand loyalty.
-Paid Promotions: Even little budgets can go quite far with designated advertisements via social media platforms.

2. Center around Local Search Engine Optimization

Upgrading your online presence for local inquiry is basic for small businesses serving a particular geographic region.
-Make a Google My Business profile.
-Use area-based keywords in your website content.
-Urge fulfilled customers to leave online reviews.

3. Assemble an Email List

Email marketing is one of the most financially cost-effective ways of sustaining leads and holding customers.
-Offer motivations like limits or free assets in return for email recruits.
-Utilize free or minimal expense email marketing platforms, for example, Mailchimp or Convert Kit to send pamphlets, advancements, and updates.

4. Work together with Others

Joining forces with correlative businesses can assist the two players with contacting new audiences.
-Have joint occasions or online courses.
-Get advance items or services through shared marketing materials.

5. Reuse Existing Content
Augment the worth of your content by adjusting it for various arrangements. For instance:
-Transform blog entries into social media bits.
-Convert customer testimonials into video testimonials.
-Use online course accounts as lead magnets.

6. Use Free Devices and Assets
Numerous internet-based apparatuses give free or reasonable answers for small companies, including:
-Canva: For designing illustrations and marketing materials.
-HubSpot CRM: For managing customer connections and marketing endeavors.
-Hootsuite: For designing social media posts.

Staying away from Common Spending Traps
Indeed, even with a very organized budget, unfortunate choices can prompt squandered assets. To guarantee your marketing dollars are spent smartly, keeping away from these normal pitfalls is fundamental:
1. Neglecting to Set Clear Measurements
Without quantifiable KPIs, deciding the progress of your campaigns is unimaginable. Define measurements, for example, transformation rates, website traffic, or customer obtaining costs at the beginning.

2. Extending Assets Excessively Far
Endeavoring to focus on each channel all the while frequently prompts weakened results. All things considered, focus your endeavors on the most significant platforms for your business.

3. Over-Dependence on Paid Advertisement
While paid promotions can convey fast outcomes, they're not a substitute for natural development strategies like Internet optimization or content marketing. Differentiate your way of dealing with guaranteed long-term manageability.

4. Disregarding Information Bits of knowledge
Numerous businesses gather information yet neglect to follow up on it. Consistently review analysis to refine your systems and try not to rehash ineffectual campaigns.

5. Underrating Time Expenses
Marketing exercises call for investment as well as cash. For instance, running a blog or managing social media records might be free yet demand predictable effort. Plan for the human resources expected to successfully execute your techniques.

6. Disregarding Testing and Cycle
Skipping A/B testing or neglecting to try different things with various strategies can bring about botched chances to streamline performance.

The Way to More Intelligent Spending

A very much oversaw marketing budget is in excess of a monetary arrangement — it's a device for accomplishing practical development. By apportioning assets insightfully, utilizing minimal expense strategies, and staying away from normal traps, businesses can extend their budgets while boosting leverage.

In marketing, achievement frequently depends not on the amount you spend, but rather on how astutely you spend it. Adjusting imagination with analysis, and procedure with adaptability, guarantees your marketing endeavors convey quantifiable and enduring outcomes.

CHAPTER 16: SCALING YOUR DIGITAL MARKETING EFFORTS

Scaling your digital marketing endeavors is fundamental for supported business development. It includes growing your span as well as improving your strategies to guarantee reliable and quantifiable achievement. Development isn't just about accomplishing more — it's tied in with doing it more smartly. To scale effectively, businesses should carry out strategies that encourage consistency, adapt business into new channels, and structure cooperative partnerships.

This section investigates significant systems for steady development, strategies for venturing into new digital channels, and how utilizing partnerships can enhance your marketing endeavors.

Strategies for Steady Development

Consistency is a sign of effective digital marketing efforts. To keep up with energy, businesses should zero in on refining their cycles, following performance, and utilizing information-driven experiences.

1. Center around Core Qualities

Recognize which marketing strategies have conveyed the best return for money invested and twofold down on those endeavors. For example:

Assuming social media crusades drive the most commitment, dispense more assets to making top-notch content for those platforms.

In the event that email marketing is your most grounded lead generator, extend your email list and improve your campaigns.

2. Automate and Streamline Processes

Mechanization is basic for adaptability. Use apparatuses to save time while keeping up with quality:

Email Automation: Platforms like Mailchimp or HubSpot can send designated emails in light of customer conduct.

Social media Designing: Devices like Hootsuite or Support assist with booking posts ahead of time, guaranteeing steady happy conveyance.

Customer Relationship Management (CRM): Frameworks like Salesforce or Zoho improve lead following and customer partnerships.

3. Carry out an Information-Driven Approach

Depending on analysis permits you to refine techniques and scale with certainty.
-Track measurements like change rates, customer obtaining expenses, and lifetime esteem.
-Use bits of knowledge to change crusades and designate assets to high-performing regions.
-Routinely lead A/B testing to figure out what reverberates most with your audience.

4. Put resources into Your Group

Scaling frequently requires extra aptitude. Consider:
-Recruiting professionals in Internet optimization, content creation, or paid publicizing.
-Giving preparation to upskill your current group in the most recent digital marketing apparatuses and strategies.

5. Keep up with Brand Identity

Development ought to never come to the detriment of brand consistency. Guarantee your information, tone, and visuals stay lined up with your basic beliefs as you scale your campaigns.

Venturing into New Digital Channels

As your business develops, expanding your digital presence can open new audiences and income streams. Be that as it may, the expansion should be vital to try not to extend assets excessively far.

1. Distinguish Opportunities for Development

Research platforms and channels that line up with your ideal interest group. For example:
-Video Marketing: Platforms like YouTube or TikTok take into consideration inventive narrating and audience commitment.
-Podcasting: Ideal for thought initiative and specialty audience focusing on.
-Arising Social Platforms: Investigate more current platforms like Strings or specialty networks like Reddit for undiscovered opportunities.

2. Explore different avenues regarding Paid Media

Extend your paid publicizing endeavors to incorporate new configurations or platforms:
-Show Marketing: Google Display Network can show your brand across a large number of websites.
-Automatic Publicizing: Use artificial intelligence-driven platforms to consequently put designated advertisements.
-Local Publicizing: Flawlessly incorporate promotions into content on platforms like Taboola or Outbrain.

3. Take on Omnichannel Marketing
-Guarantee your marketing endeavors give a consistent encounter across all platforms.
-Make brought together informing that Sales with email, social media, websites, and applications.
-Use retargeting strategies to draw in customers who associate with your content across various channels.

4. Explore International Business sectors

Extending geologically is one more method for scaling:
-Enhance your website and content for multilingual audiences.

-Utilize local influencers or partnerships to lay out believability in new locales.
-Research Local Search engine optimization and marketing platforms well-defined for your objective business sectors.

5. Gain on Trends and Innovations

Remain on the ball by taking on arising advances, for example,
-Computer-based intelligence and AI: Utilize prescient analysis to figure out customer conduct.
-Voice Inquiry Advancement: Adjust content for platforms like Alexa or Google Associate.
-Intelligent Content: Integrate tests, reviews, and expanded reality encounters.

Utilizing Partnerships and Collaborations

Partnerships can speed up development by permitting you to take advantage of new audiences and offer assets. Cooperative endeavors are cost-effective and can fortify your brand's standing.

1. Recognize Key Partnerships

Search for businesses or leverages whose audience covers yours yet doesn't straightforwardly contend. Models include:
-A wellness brand joining forces with a good food organization.
-A SaaS platform working together with a digital marketing organization.

2. Co-Make Content

Coordinated efforts can intensify your range while sharing the responsibility.
-Have joint online classes or live occasions with industry specialists.
-Make co-marked digital books, guides, or video series.
-Cross-advance content on one another's foundation.

3. Affiliate and Referral Programs

Boost different businesses or people to advance your items or services.
-Offer com campaigns or limits for fruitful references.
-Use associate businesses like ShareASale or Rakuten to extend your compass.

4. Leverage Influencer Marketing

Influencers can introduce your brand to their devotees in a bona fide manner.
-Center around miniature leverages with connected specialty audiences.
-Foster long-term partnerships as opposed to one-off campaigns for more prominent trust and effect.

5. Participate in Industry Unions

Join industry affiliations, gatherings, or systems administration gatherings. These platforms give potential opportunities to:
-Information sharing and remaining refreshed on patterns.

-Teaming up for bigger scope campaigns or drives.

Scaling your digital marketing endeavors isn't tied in with pursuing each opportunity — it's tied in with adjusting development systems to your business objectives. Consistency, determined expansion, and joint effort are the foundations of maintainable development.

By zeroing in on high-leverage strategies, analyzing undiscovered channels, and utilizing the power of partnerships, you can hoist your digital presence without overpowering your assets.

Conclusion

Digital marketing offers entrepreneurs an incredible opportunity to extend their range, interface with their main interest group, and drive development — all without requiring enormous budgets. Through this book, we've investigated fundamental systems for building major areas of strength for a presence, attracting people to your website, converting guests into customers, and supporting long-term achievement.

From putting forth Cost-effective objectives and understanding your audience to utilizing local search engine optimization, social media, and email marketing, the instruments and strategies talked about give noteworthy platforms to improve your digital presence. Keep in mind, that analysis is your compass, conducting you to refine campaigns given genuine information, while a very much arranged marketing budget guarantees assets are distributed for the greatest effect. Scaling endeavors and embracing new digital channels will additionally situate your business for reliable development.

Right now is an ideal opportunity to act. Begin by executing even one strategy from this book to start changing your marketing endeavors. Remain reliable, stay versatile, and keep on testing. Progress in digital marketing is a journey, not an objective, and your commitment will prompt enduring outcomes.

As you push ahead, let this book act as your guide for exploring the steadily developing digital scene. Your small business has the ability to flourish — embrace the strategies, make a move, and leave your imprint on the internet!